Florida
Florida
FLORIDA
FLORIDA
FLORIDA
FLORIDA
FLORIDA
Florid
Florida
FLORIDA

FLORIDA FLORIDA

FLORIDA FLORIDA

FLORIDA

FLORIDA FLORIDA

FLORIDA

Florida FLORIDA

BORN & RAISED
IN FLORIDA

Only in Florida

IT'S RAINING IGUANAS IN FL TODAY!

TODAY'S FORECAST:

BRACE YOURSELVES! *WINTER* ISN'T COMING.

FLORIDA SWEETHEART CALADIUM

LEAVENWORTH'S TICKSEED

BLANKET FLOWER

ALLIGATORLILY

BUTTERFLY WEED

WILD POTATO MORNING GLORY

SKYBLUE CLUSTERVINE

SUNSHINE MIMOSA

PURPLE CONEFLOWER

BEACH SUNFLOWER

DOLE WHIP

CORTADITO

STONE CRABS

PINK SHRIMP

RUM CAKE

CUBANO

CONCH FRITTERS

KEY LIME PIE

GUAVA PASTELITO

PUBLIX SUB

FRIED GATOR BITES

TALLAHASSEE
JACKSONVILLE
INTERSTATE
10
FLORIDA
US
441
INTERSTATE
FLORIDA
95
OCALA
DAYTONA BEACH
19
INTERSTATE
FLORIDA
4
ORLANDO
FLORIDA'S TURNPIKE
TAMPA
LAKELAND
ST. PETERSBURG
17
INTERSTATE
FLORIDA
275
INTERSTATE
FLORIDA
75
27
Welcome to
FLORIDA
THE SUNSHINE STATE
NAPLES
1
MIAMI

KEY WEST LIGHTHOUSE

SOUTH FLORIDA

Gulf Coast

Sunshine Skyway Bridge

TAMPA

Big Cypress Swamp

Mermaids of Weeki Wachee

The Dali Museum

Crystal River

St. Petersburg

SARASOTA

Marco Island

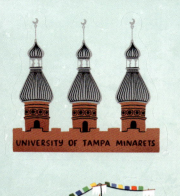

Central Florida

Orlando

BOK TOWER GARDENS

Daytona Beach

Winter Garden

LAKELAND

I ♥ MICKEY

BEST DAY EVER

UNIVERSAL

Space Coast

Palm Bay

Kennedy Space Center

Merritt Island

Cocoa Beach

Florida

Titusville

Port Canaveral

Melbourne

NORTH FLORIDA

JACKSONVILLE

GINNIE SPRINGS

Gainesville

OCALA *National Forest*

St. Augustine

Palm Coast

OCALA

Amelia Island